GOD BLESS YOU

IT'S NEVER
Too
LATE

Also by William Moss

FINDING INNER PEACE DURING TROUBLED TIMES

It's Never Too Late

My Spiritual Journey

William Moss

PREFACE by Senator John C. Danforth
FOREWORD by (The Rev.) Curtis G. Almquist SSJE
INTRODUCTION by George H. W. Bush

Glitterati
INCORPORATED
New York | London

First published in 2012 by

Glitterati Incorporated
New York | London

New York Office:
225 Central Park West
New York, New York 10022
Telephone: 212 362 9119

London Office:
1 Rona Road
London NW3 2HY
Tel/Fax +44 (0) 207 267 9739

www.GlitteratiIncorporated.com
media@GlitteratiIncorporated.com for inquiries

First edition, 2012

Library of Congress Cataloging-in-Publication data is
available from the publisher.

Hardcover edition ISBN 978-0-9832702-9-4
Editor: Eveline Chao
Illustrations: Amanda McGough
Design: Sarah Morgan Karp/smk-design.com

Printed and bound in China

10 9 8 7 6 5 4 3 2 1

CONTENTS

IF YOU HAVE ANY CONCERNS ABOUT DRINKING... THEN THIS BOOK IS *for you.*

ACKNOWLEDGMENTS

I want to thank Dr. Garrett O'Connor, Dr. James West, Reverend William J. A. Power, and (The Rev.) Curtis G. Almquist SSJE for their contributions to my life and this book.

And a special thank you to Senator John C. Danforth, and President George H. W. Bush for their inspiration and support. And of course, my wife Dianne, whom I will love forever. Thanks as well to my assistant, Mona Pollina, who helped me with this book, and to editor Eveline Chao, illustrator Amanda McGough, and designer Sarah Morgan Karp who each contributed to the project.

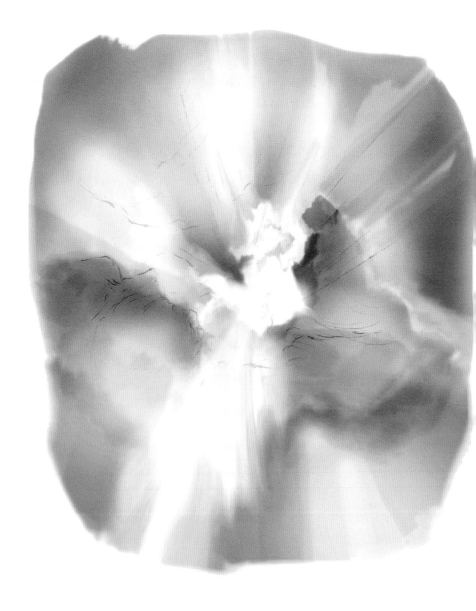

Preface

---·•◦•·---

Senator John C. Danforth

*F*riends who have known Bill Moss for more than six years speak of an astonishing change since he was a mere eighty-five. They say he was as always bright, kind, and friendly as he is today, that he had an interesting but extremely complicated lifestyle, was restless, at times drank too much, and sometimes seemed to be distracted by personal problems and, in that sense that he is now a different person. The new Bill Moss is a life force, offering hope to countless people, many of whom he has never met. That this change occurred in the midst of his ninth decade explains the title, *It's Never Too Late*.

This book is the story of the power of God and the candidly admitted frailty of a man, and of how after much struggle the one overcame the other. What changed wasn't God's love for Bill. That has been a constant throughout Bill's life. What changed was Bill's response to God's love.

Since childhood, it seemed to him that God was trying to get his attention, not whispering to him as in the still small voice that spoke to Elijah, but fairly shouting in his ear. On two occasions, extended business meetings forced Bill to miss flights on which he had been booked. Each time, the plane crashed, killing all aboard. Then there were numerous drunk-driving episodes that he survived. Bill is convinced that God had intervened in these situations to spare his life, so that he might serve some useful purpose. But, however sure that God had spared him for a purpose, Bill did little in response.

His story of a wildly drunken drive down a winding mountain road is revealing. He writes, "As I flew down the side of that mountain, taking curves at seventy-five miles an hour, I could feel the steady hand of God on the steering wheel." It's an admission of passivity as well as irresponsibility. What a remarkable division of labor: I'll do the drinking and leave the driving to God.

So what changed in Bill at age eighty-five? Precisely *what* is never too late? I think the answer Bill gives can be summed up in one word: "action." For a lifetime, he had pondered what purpose God might have meant for him. Now it was time to stop pondering and start doing. It does not suffice to think that God exists, or even to believe that God is acting in our lives, because faith isn't merely a matter of the mind. It isn't passive. It requires us to do something. Jesus didn't ask his disciples to think good thoughts about him; he told them to get moving, to leave their nets and follow him. This is the call Bill Moss heard in a Laguna, California bar – an authentic religious experience, "as though lightning flashed and thunder struck in a moment of complete clarity." The time had come when it was no longer enough to wonder, passively, if God had some purpose for his life. The moment had come to start acting.

That's just what Bill began doing, first by getting and staying sober, then by reaching out to other alcoholics, by writing books helpful to struggling souls—*Finding Peace in Troubled Times* and this book—then by appearing on radio programs. All of this began at age eighty-five.

Bill Moss has told me that it's a wonderful thing to have a new project in the last years of life. He has quite a project going – not just thinking like a Christian, but acting like one. If it's a new project for him, it can be a new project for each of us: turning our life around. We call it repentance. As Bill teaches us, it's never too late for such a project. Never.

John C. Danforth served as a United States Senator from Missouri for eighteen years and is an ordained Episcopal priest.

FOREWORD

———•◦•———

(THE REV.)
CURTIS G. ALMQUIST SSJE

So many things in life come to their end. Business ventures are clinched or failed, and life moves on. Hollywood productions have their runs; trees and plants come to fruition and then go to seed; our relationships with family, friends, and colleagues change and die over time. Some of these changes in life will give us great joy, gladness, and thanksgiving. Some of these changes in life will leave us full of sorrow or regret. If only we knew then what we know now, life would be different.

But that's not the way life works. All of this – the best and the worst of life's experiences – form a reservoir in the depths of the human soul. And yet in the grand scheme of things God the Creator is very frugal, wasting nothing. So all of human life is like an oil field waiting to be tapped, a treasure waiting to be discovered within the soul. The treasure is tapped by love.

In this metaphor, Bill Moss is the perfect treasure. He has been spent, done, gone, lost at the bottom of the sea and then he has been redeemed, and turned into a treasure. He has been tapped by the love of his wife, his family, his friends – all of whom have mirrored the love of God into the deep recesses of his soul. And what is gushing out of him now, through this book and his other writings, his deeds, his essential self, is the soul of a lifetime. It's the success of an oilman, a producer, a writer, an entrepreneur, a friend of the mighty and the broken, a father and a husband. In this season of his lifetime he is more than all else a great lover of God, and a man at peace. His fullness of time has come and through the heartfelt words and story here, he brings this incredible gift and knowledge to others in need. He shows us that it is never too late to find the way.

Curtis G. Almquist is an Episcopal priest of the Society of Saint John the Evangelist, Cambridge, MA, a monastic community of The Episcopal Church.

INTRODUCTION

———•◆•———

GEORGE H. W. BUSH

I am not sure when I met Bill Moss. At age eighty-seven I really can't remember when I met anyone anymore, except of course for Barbara. But it seems I have known Bill almost forever – for at least as long as I have lived in the great state of Texas.

He's always been a great friend, and when I needed him, a great supporter. Bill Moss is one of those people that when I look back, I realize without him and his support, I likely would have never been President of the United States. He was always there for me, working tirelessly to raise money, to raise awareness, and to raise votes. And in return, he never asked for anything. His friendship was always given freely and generously.

My memories of Bill back then were that he was a very successful businessman who certainly knew how to enjoy life. Neither Barbara nor I had any idea of the struggles he had with alcohol, or that at times he felt he had lost his way. I don't think anyone suspected his troubles. Which in many ways, makes his sharing of his very personal journey in *It's Never Too Late* even more amazing. There was no compelling reason for Bill to share his private journey of faith – he owed no one any explanations of any kind. But typical of Bill and his very generous nature, he felt he had to share his story of struggle and triumph and eventually, peace.

My guess is that his story will touch many hearts, and perhaps save a soul or two. His message of returning to God and fully realizing and living his faith is both powerful and inspirational. My way of trying to prove "it's never too late" is to jump out of perfectly good airplanes. Bill's way is to open his heart.

Barbara and I are proud to call Bill and his wonderful wife Dianne dear friends. They have enriched our lives in ways hard to explain but which you will understand better when you read *It's Never Too Late*.

George H. W. Bush is the forty-first President of the United States (1989-1993).

PRELUDE

---•◦•---

*M*y name is Bill Moss; I'm sitting on the patio of our cottage in Indian Wells, California. It is winter but the weather is beautiful, snow-capped mountains in the background, lush green grass, a gentle breeze, a warm sun, and billowy white clouds. I'm ninety-one years old and I'm thinking about my relationship with God. It has been a tussle. God has been steadfast. I have not.

I had been thinking of writing my life story but instead I am going to write about my lifelong relationship with God. The first three chapters, The Early Years, Riding High, and The Road Home, when I was chasing dreams, represent the part of my life that helped me find God's plan for me. The last three chapters, Finding God, Understanding God, and Doing God's Work, contain scriptures, prayers, meditations, and reflections that guided me in turning my will and my life over to the care of God.

THE EARLY YEARS

---

*M*y spiritual journey actually began when I was a little redheaded kid growing up in Odessa, a dusty little town in West Texas, where my mother was very active in the Baptist church and my father was the city attorney.

One Sunday morning when I was eleven or twelve years old, as the choir quietly sang "Just as I Am, without One Plea," I became a member of the Baptist church. Later, when I was baptized, by immersion, I thought the preacher was going to let me drown. He didn't, and I became a Christian.

A couple of years later at a Baptist summer encampment with my mother, more than 200 people came by car over simple country roads. The encampment was under a canopy of trees situated on the colorful banks of Limpia Creek. It was cool and delightful in the extraordinary Davis Mountains of the Big Bend country in West Texas. We went to religious services in the morning, at lunch, and in the evening. It was a very emotional experience and one I will remember forever.

At one service the preacher, at his Baptist best, was exhorting the congregation to contribute to the expenses of the encampment. I found my thirteen-year-old self walking down the center aisle and up onto the stage, where, standing by the preacher, I announced I was giving a calf. The reaction was explosive – the "widow's mite" the preacher proclaimed, referring to a bible verse that tells us that the contribution of someone with very little is worth more than that from someone with a lot. I was very proud and got a standing ovation.

Back in Odessa my father sternly reminded me that since I had only two calves I had given the preacher one-half of my herd.

We met a counselor at the encampment from San Marcos Baptist Academy, a school in Central Texas. The next fall I enrolled in boarding school at San Marcos. We attended chapel every day, went to Sunday school and church, and asked the blessing at every meal. I felt I was a devout Christian.

A Boy on a Horse

During the summer vacation my dad put me in a pick-up and took me to a ranch we had in the Sacramento Mountains of New Mexico. Our ranch headquarters were thirty miles from the nearest town. We were isolated.

I had a horse that I loved. On Sundays I would saddle my horse and ride several miles into the mountains to a beautiful spring. It was within a forest permit where we ran cattle as part of the ranch operation. I would tie my horse to the fence and walk out to the top of an escarpment from which I could see far into the distance, across the New Mexico white sands and beyond to the Organ Mountains. On a clear day, I could see all the way to El Paso. As a sixteen-year-old cowboy, I was absorbed by the wonder of it all, and curious about the lives of the people down below. I wondered what would become of me? What would my life be like? I enjoyed the solitude, and the majesty of the Creator. It expanded the horizons of my life. When I think of it today I remember how peaceful it was. There was beauty in my soul; I was in the presence of God. It was like a prayer come to life. The mystery and magnificence created emotions in me that I had not experienced before. I had a spiritual experience that would last a lifetime. I knew my life was in God's hands.

At dusk when I got back on my horse, I only had to wrap the reins around the saddle horn, jangle my spurs, and sit back in the saddle. My horse knew the way home.

College

After finishing San Marcos Baptist Academy I went to Baylor University in Waco, Texas where I had my first drink. My life changed. Girls, dancing, and football trips to other schools took precedence over studying. It took me five years to graduate with a degree in drama and speech. Along the way I took some courses in religion and even thought about becoming a minister. I dreamed of being a writer and making the world a better place. I'm sure that God was calling me but the lure of booze and parties was pulling me in another direction. I ran with the popular crowd and was recognized all over the campus. I was having a helluva good time. I studied drama and played leads at the Baylor University Theatre as I prepared for a career on the stage or in movies.

World War II started. I volunteered for the Air Corps but because of my poor vision, was discharged. I came back and finished Baylor and was drafted into the Army, where I developed an ulcer, received a medical discharge, and was off to Hollywood to become an actor and a writer. It was my thought that motion pictures were a platform to express my thoughts as to making the world a better place. I wonder if all this was part of God's plan for me.

RIDING HIGH

◆━◆━◆

HOLLYWOOD

*I*n Hollywood I had an introduction to the secretary of the casting director at Paramount Pictures. She introduced me to an actor's agent. I worked and supported myself as an actor for three or four years. I had small parts in fifteen movies between 1943 and 1947. I was never a star in pictures but I was a star along the Sunset Strip, with its glitter and glamour, paparazzi and starlets, night clubs and great restaurants. I produced a successful Technicolor movie and had the opportunity to continue as a producer with major studios.

I married a former child star and we had three children. I was operating the family ranch in New Mexico and dabbling in the oil business in Texas. I moved back to Odessa to provide a more stable background for my family. Oil had been discovered on a ranch my father had purchased just outside of Odessa. He was busy practicing law and needed help in the oil business.

BUSINESS

After working with my dad for about a year, I recognized that some of the insecurities and feelings that I had had in my relationship with him as a younger person were reoccurring. There was no real warmth. I did not receive recognition or approval of the work I was doing. I decided that I would go into business for myself. So I moved to Midland, Texas where most of the oil company's executive offices were.

During the next thirty years my business flourished. I started at the very bottom hawking oil deals that I generated and assembled. I was able to attract outstanding geologists by giving them a piece of the action. I made enough cash to cover my living expenses and negotiated an interest in each prospect as part of my fee. That was the beginning of my success. My geologist continued working in the Midland office but I moved to Dallas where there was a more active market for my deals. I made lifelong friends in the oil business, had an active social life and a helluva good time. I did not recognize God in my life. My drinking continued.

It did not take me long to learn that some of the oilmen in Dallas were getting their financing in New York. So I rented an apartment in New York City, opened a financial office there, and with the help of investment bankers raised a lot of drilling money. New York City became vital to my expanding oil business, as did contacts I made in Palm Beach, Florida, where I leased a home in the winter, and Southampton, New York, where I leased a home in the summer.

I got the best tables in the great restaurants and famous night clubs. Not because I was famous but because I was a big tipper. Entertaining was an integral part of my business. My life became a whirlwind of parties, private jets, chartered yachts, and memberships in many exclusive private clubs. There were elegant and entertaining ladies with whom I made some lasting friendships and had a few misguided romances. I went to Wimbledon, the U.S. Open tennis, U.S. Open golf, The Masters, Super Bowls, the World Series, the theatre, ballet, symphonies, and the Oscars. There were always cocktails before business lunches, drinks before dinner, wine with dinner, and on special occasions, champagne and caviar. Sometimes we went to a floor show after dinner. It was what most of my friends and business associates enjoyed as a way of life. We joked about hangovers and went on our merry way.

One day a friend of mine arranged an appointment for me in New York with a senior member of a big investment firm. I was on time but he kept me waiting for nearly an hour. When I finally got in to see him our meeting was encouraging and lasted longer than expected. I had a plane to catch. When I left his office I got caught up in the traffic of a parade for astronaut John Glenn, who earlier that year had become the first American to orbit the Earth. I missed the plane. I went back across the street to the office of a friend of mine who knew I was supposed to be on that flight. When he saw me, his face turned white. My missed plane was American Flight 1, which crashed shortly after takeoff on March 1, 1962. All eighty-seven passengers and eight crew died.

I was working hard and my companies were financially successful. We were finding and developing oil and gas, developing real estate, and making and selling other investments. I was making millions of dollars but my lifestyle was expensive, excessive, and permissive. I was experiencing anxiety and stress, drinking a lot and taking sedatives to sleep. I put tremendous pressure on myself to succeed and be accepted. Although my main office, with its growing staff, had remained in Dallas, I had exploration offices in Midland and Houston, Texas; Lafayette, Louisiana; and Jackson Mississippi. I was too busy for church and drifted farther away from God.

On May 3, 1968 I had an important business meeting in Houston which ran overtime because of some protracted negotiations. Once again I missed a flight. This time, it was Braniff Flight 352 from Houston to Dallas. It crashed and everyone on board was killed.

After each crash I believed that God had saved my life and wondered if He had something left for me to do.

POLITICS

I became active in Republican politics, spending part of my time in Washington, D.C. I began making contributions to the Republican National Committee and Senate races. At events I attended, I not only met politicians but also the fundraising staffs that supported them. It became evident to me that it is easy to get into political fundraising, if you have money, an airplane, and wealthy friends. I had all three. So I became active in the Republican National Committee, Senate races, and Presidential campaigns. It was exciting and stimulating. The events were at interesting places, and there were always cocktails, music, and ambitious people.

In 1980 at the National Republican Convention in Detroit, Michigan, when Ronald Reagan received the presidential nomination, I was with my friend George Bush when he was selected to run for Vice President. I was lucky to have met George and Barbara in Midland Texas in the '50s when we were struggling to get started in the oil business.

The election of Reagan and Bush in 1980 brought great promise and excitement to Washington, and the social life to new heights. Electricity was in the air. Invitations to elegant State dinners and the White House were sought after with a vengeance. I was caught up in it. Meeting interesting and dedicated people from all over the world. The social life that goes with national politics can be exhilarating.

I was invited to be on the Board of Trustees, served as chairman of the Finance and Investment Committee, and was a member of the Executive Committee at American University in Washington, D.C. I organized The William Moss Institute, a think tank at American University.

I also founded and chaired the Television Corporation of America, which produced the Peabody Award-winning "748 Days that Changed America," concerning Nixon's inauguration, Watergate, and his resignation.

It was during this time that I first consulted a psychiatrist about my drinking. I had frightened myself after a long night of drinking by consuming a bottle of wine while driving at night from Southampton to New York City on the Long Island Expressway. There were many times that I drove after drinking and it's a miracle that I did not have a terrible accident. I could have killed somebody. I am convinced that God was looking after me.

After some weeks with the psychiatrist, who was an addiction specialist of great renown, he concluded that I was not an alcoholic but a heavy social drinker who could quit when I wanted to. Of course this thrilled me and I went straight to the famous 21 Club and bought drinks for the house. I could stop drinking for short periods of time but my business, politics, and social life kept me involved with places, parties, and events where drinking was so prevalent that I always gradually slipped back into it. So I went to health spas a couple of times a year to "go on the wagon," lose weight, and exercise.

One Sunday in Scottsdale, Arizona, while I was at John Gardiner's Tennis Ranch for a U.S. Senate charity event, I drove into the mountains and on the way back I stopped at a bar to watch a Dallas Cowboys football game, where I had several martinis. I got drunk. The highway out of the mountains back to Scottsdale was a winding, precipitous road along the side of the mountains. As I flew down the side of that mountain, taking curves at seventy-five miles an hour, I could feel the steady hand of God on the steering wheel. I felt as if I was in His warm glow of love. I felt certain that I would arrive in Scottsdale safely, and I did.

I thank God for saving my life so many times. Was it a part of His plan for me? Would there be an opportunity in the future to hear a call to His service?

———— ·•· ————

During the George H. W. Bush campaign for President, I served as vice chairman of the National Finance Committee, and was on the National Steering Committee. I also organized his first fundraiser in 1979 when he was running for the nomination. Later, when he was elected President, I was co-chairman of one of the inaugural balls.

After he was elected, the President asked me to serve as chairman of his Drug Advisory Council which was part of the Executive Office of the President. At that time, some polls showed the cause and effect of drug use was the number-one concern in the country. The Council was formed to advise the President on ways to involve the private sector in the war on drugs. Thirty nationally recognized individuals from business, labor, education, community organizations, and the press served on the Council. Meetings and seminars were held in the White House with leaders of community, religious and service organizations, educators, and labor. The recommendations made to the President at a meeting at Camp David on November 15, 1991 led to the merger of two of the Council's private organizations: Coalitions against Drug Abuse and Drugs Don't Work. These organizations were later merged into the Community Anti-Drug Coalitions of America (CADCA). CADCA is currently operating in all 50 states and more than 1,500 communities across the nation, and is expanding internationally into South America and Africa.

He also appointed me to the National Petroleum Council.

Why was politics so seductive to me? The scramble for recognition, helping the country, the stimulation, basking in reflective glory, the exhilaration of being in the

Oval Office, knowing senators and Cabinet members on a first-name basis, lunch at the White House mess, embassy parties, inaugural balls, contacts with the high and mighty, trips to Camp David, the feeling of being at the center of power; all of this was a long way from the dusty little town of Odessa, Texas.

Having a good, loyal, longtime friend as President of the United States is an experience that very, very few people understand. Things like a movie in the White House, coffee on the Truman balcony, meetings in the Roosevelt room, dinners with the President and the First Lady at local restaurants, knowing when they are sick or not feeling good, loving them just for their personal characteristics, knowing unconditional friendships, having the opportunity to serve the highest office in the land, are indescribable. I thank God for providing me with this great experience.

When George Bush was not re-elected, Washington was not the same for me. I realized that if you don't have a position of prominence in Washington, or if you're not fully engaged in political activities, that Washington could be a lonely place.

In December of 1994, I was having lunch alone at my favorite table at the exclusive Jockey Club, with my usual martinis, and reflecting on the life I had had in business, socially, and in politics.

Something was missing in my life. There had been no real peace or tranquility, and very little happiness. I did not have the loving relationship with my kids that I longed for. Drinking, traveling, and the life I led had contributed to four shattered marriages.

What had I done with my life? I wondered what had become of the redheaded kid that had given half his herd to the preacher. The sixteen-year-old cowboy with his horse and a vision. The college freshman who considered being a minister. A young writer who wanted to make the world a better place. All before booze and parties took over and my craving for recognition, wealth, and acceptance had set in. I realized the music had stopped playing. I felt alone.

I was seventy-four years old.

I was riding high. I had accomplished so much…and yet so little.

It was time for me to return to Texas. So I came home to Dallas.

I sold my apartment in New York and let the leases in Palm Beach and Southampton expire. By the time I returned to Dallas, I had sold The Petroleum Corporation, William Moss Oil Corp., my office building, ranches, and farms, and had invested the money. I still had the income from my oil and gas royalties.

I had time on my hands. In Dallas, I began roaming around looking for a new life. I occasionally went to church and began to think and pray a little about how I could fit into a life with God. I supported an evangelist who had a weekly radio program in Palm Desert, California. I had begun keeping a journal with thoughts about my religion and how I might serve God. I went occasionally to Presbyterian, Methodist, and community churches, looking for a home for my lonely soul.

The Road Home

---•◆•---

"Enter through the narrow gate. For wide is the gate and broad is the road that leads to destruction, and many enter through it. But small is the gate and narrow the road that leads to life, and only a few find it."

—MATTHEW 7:13-14

DIANNE

In January of 1995 a good friend, whom we had both known for years, introduced me to Dianne Van Horn Ingels. She was completely different from any other woman that I had ever met. She had a beautiful heart full of love, was devoted to God, and was the most thoughtful person I had ever met. She had a great sense of humor, intelligent, was well read, and enjoyed a very successful business and political career. We had similar interests, liked the same things, the same people, and the same challenges. On our second date she asked if I was spiritual, and it was like an epiphany. I said "yes." We both agreed that God had brought us together.

Dianne is the most beautiful women I have ever met and after living with her for fifteen years, I am convinced that she is one of God's angels and the greatest woman I have ever known. She is the best thing that ever happened to me. When we married in Beaver Creek, Colorado on Christmas Day in 1995, our lives changed forever.

Dianne and I had a condominium in Dallas and also bought a cottage at The Vintage Club in Indian Wells, California, which suited us perfectly.

As part of our life together we met Reverend William J. A. Power who was a Professor of Theology at Southern Methodist University and Associate Rector at Saint Michael and All Angels Episcopal Church in Dallas. He changed my life. He became a mentor and spiritual director to me, as well as one of my closest friends. Dianne and I joined the Episcopal Church so we could worship together. Through Saint Michael, Bill Power arranged for me to attend a retreat at the Monastery of the Society of Saint John the Evangelist in Cambridge, Massachusetts. There I met (The Rev.) Curtis Almquist, a monk, who also became a spiritual adviser and loving friend, and who helped me understand my relationship with God and the power of prayer and meditation. I will be forever grateful to Bill Power.

We traveled to the Holy Land and became interested in the plight of the Palestinian Christians. We had met and worked with the Reverend Canon John L. Peterson, the first Canon for Global Justice and Reconciliation at Washington National Cathedral. Our work for the Palestinian Christians included meetings with George H. W. Bush, James and Susan Baker, Brent Scowcroft, and others.

THE WIDE GATE

By the fall and early winter of 2005 my drinking had intensified to the point that it had become a real problem. I had tried over and over again, but could not quit drinking. Once again, another psychiatrist to whom I went for consultation told me that I did not need treatment. So I decided to take a week or ten days and go back to the Montage resort and spa in Laguna Beach, California, where I could "go on the wagon," walk on the beach, work out in the gym, get massages in the spa, and go on a diet to lose weight. Before leaving our cottage in Indian Wells I decided to have lunch at the Club. I had two martinis before lunch and some wine with lunch. When I got back to our cottage I saw a bottle of Beefeater gin sitting on the bar. I got a 16-ounce plastic cup, put in some ice, and filled it with the gin.

I had a limo to take me to Laguna so I sat blissfully in the backseat, leisurely sipping my gin during the two-hour trip. When we got to the hotel, it was my custom to go directly to my suite and begin my regimen, but this time I went to the bar and ordered a Beefeater martini, shaken-not-stirred, served in a chilled stem glass with a twist. It was beautiful.

Before I finished my second martini, it became crystal clear to me that if I continued it would be total disaster, it would be the end. Drinking had finally caught up with me. My life could be over. I could become a worthless drunk and lose everything. I could not recover. Booze would kill me if I did not kill myself first. It was as though lightning flashed and thunder struck in a moment of complete clarity. God was pulling me back from the brink of total disaster. I had let the bugles blow, the band play on, the horses run, while I dithered away parts of my time here on Earth. I had not listened to God. I was completely defeated. I was powerless over alcohol and my life had become unmanageable.

God had led me to heights that I did not expect to find before He decided to let me fall over the precipice of an alcoholic cliff where the broad road ended. Death flashed before my eyes when I hit the rocky bottom of the cliff. I had hit my alcoholic bottom. He saved my life. I turned my life and will over to the care of God. I completely surrendered to God's will.

My soul was still intact, my heart still strong, and my vision clear enough to see the mistakes I had made. In spite of my many excesses, God offered His hand to save me from the destruction of the life I had lived with a drink in my hand, and began to show me a life of sobriety. The life He had planned for me all along. A new life I could never have found by myself. God was holding me softly in His arms, with complete love, His warmth and strength absolute. His caring sublime. I can still feel the floating sensation of

Heaven. I heard Him say faintly in the distance, "I forgive you…I forgive you." He was offering me hope, a chance to pick up the spiritual life that I had left in college.

I was eighty-five years old.

After a while I heard Him say, "Call your friend Betty Ford." Betty Ford graciously introduced me to Dr. Garrett O'Connor. Dr. O'Connor was, at the time, the Chief Psychiatrist at the Betty Ford Center, and internationally considered one of the best in his field. He had years of experience in helping patients grapple with the disease of alcoholism. Rather than have me enroll in the Betty Ford Center, Dr. O'Connor counseled me personally and my life in sobriety began. For the first time in my life, I said, "My name is Bill and I am an alcoholic." In the ensuing years he has helped me understand the devastation of alcoholism and the importance of a higher power in finding sobriety. He has become one of the most important and caring friends in my life.

In college, I had entered the wide gate and lived on the broad road that leads to destruction and many enter through it.

Now, my life was coming together.

"So I entered the small gate and narrow road
that leads to life and only a few find it."

THE SMALL GATE

Early in my recovery I picked up my Bible and began to read it again, and a whole new spiritual world began to reveal itself to me. I realized I was at a completely new place in my life.

I began to pray. I thanked God profusely for all the wonderful things He had done for me. Places I had been, people I had met, and material successes I had enjoyed. I recognized once again that God had been guiding my life. I thanked Him over and over. I could feel His love.

I prayed for forgiveness for my many sins.

I was on the road home.

When I recognized a power greater than myself, a new spiritual journey began.

The Bible says, "Ask and it will be given you, seek and you will find, knock and the door will be open to you." This scripture opened the door for a foundation to rejoin God. It guided me in creating the new life that I so fervently desired. I realized I must recognize and accept God, surrender to Him, pray to Him, put my faith and trust in Him.

It is my prayer, with God's help, that through finding God, understanding God, loving God, and doing God's work, it's not too late to help others and make the world a better place.

I was on the narrow road.

Finding God

The Power Greater Than Ourselves

Through the process of my recovery, I learned the importance of an individual's relationship with a "power greater than ourselves." That power in my case was God. But I did not fully realize how powerful God would become in my life until I made the decision to turn my will and life over to the care of God. It all came together as my life was completely transformed at eighty-five years old when I sought through prayer and meditation to improve my conscious contact with God praying only for knowledge of His will for us and the power to carry that out.

HE WHO SEEKS GOD
HAS ALREADY FOUND HIM

My retreat at the Episcopal monastery, which had been suggested by my spiritual advisor William J. A. Power, was a deep spiritual experience, one that added another dimension to my life. There were five services a day where the monks chanted prayers and sang holy songs. We ate in silence with the monks and were taken into their hearts and souls. It was a great experience for me because I learned that he who seeks God has already found Him. But in seeking God there were steps we all need to take.

I believe it helps to find God if we open our minds, hearts and souls to His love and listen.

Can we love others as God loved us?

Can we be truthful?

Can we refuse all temptation?

Can we fully forgive?

Can we be humble rather than arrogant
  and self-serving?

Can we be understanding?

Can we have compassion for others?

Can we control our temper?

Can we be kind, gentle and patient?

Can we be non-judgmental?

Can we pray for forgiveness of our sins
  and transgressions?

Can we be grateful for the comforts and joys
  He has provided?

Can we live and work in this materialistic society and still love and trust others? Can we turn our will and lives over to the care of God and within our heart of hearts, put our faith and trust in Him? All the while thanking God for His abundant gifts, blessings, and directions He has given us.

HOLY LIVING

In finding God again and praying for ways to expand my spirituality with a new perspective, I was inspired by the holy life in the monastery. However, outside the silence of monastic life it is difficult to be constantly aware of God's holiness. Sharing the scriptures below has helped me and I believe they will help others who are grappling with alcohol and other debilitating addictions.

> *"Put to death, therefore, whatever belongs to your earthly nature: sexual immorality, impurity, lust, evil desires."*

> *"You used to walk in these ways, in the life you once lived. But now you must rid yourselves of all such things as these: anger, rage, malice, slander, and filthy language from your lips. Do not lie to each other, since you have taken off your old self with its practices and have put on the new self, which is being renewed in knowledge in the image of its Creator."*

"Therefore, clothe yourselves with compassion, kindness, humility, gentleness and patience. Bear with each other and forgive whatever grievances you may have against one another. Forgive as the Lord forgave you. And over all these virtues put on love, which binds them all together in perfect unity."

"Let the peace of Christ rule in your hearts, since as members of one body you were called to peace. And be thankful. Let the word of Christ dwell in you richly as you teach and admonish one another with all wisdom, and with gratitude to God."

I realized that to be a holy person I would have to give up worldly ambitions and serve God humbly.

My spiritual journey was taking me to a new relationship with God. I was developing a deeper more meaningful understanding of spirituality when I read:

THE LORD IS MY SHEPHERD

The LORD is my shepherd, I shall not want.

He maketh me to lie down in green pastures: he leadeth me beside the still waters.

He restoreth my soul: he leadeth me in the paths of righteousness for his name's sake.

Yea, though I walk through the valley of the shadow of death, I will fear no evil: for thou art with me; thy rod and thy staff they comfort me.

Thou preparest a table before me in the presence of mine enemies: thou anointest my head with oil; my cup runneth over.

Surely goodness and mercy will follow me all the days of my life: and I will dwell in the house of the LORD for ever.

I knew I had found the God who had saved me from disaster. I could put my faith and trust in Him as I continued my spiritual journey.

God

Understanding God

---

*"For it is by grace you have been saved,
through faith—and this not from yourselves,
it is the gift of God—not by works, so that no
one can boast. For we are God's workmanship,
created in Christ Jesus to do good works, which
God prepared in advance for us to do."*

THE INDWELLING

As a young person my mother taught me, and I heard in churches, that God was in Heaven, out there somewhere beyond our reach in the sky. He controlled the universe, the stars, the sun and the moon: rain and famine, the rivers and lakes, the ocean, skies, mountains, the world and all the people in it. But I did not understand exactly how I personally fit into this expansive picture.

These many years later I realize that for me to understand God I must welcome Him into my life. I must pray to Him to forgive me of all of my sins; to cleanse me, to prune the dead branches from the tree, and to guide me in finding and accepting His plans for me.

I talked at length with my spiritual advisors about my struggle to understand God and His plans for me. After praying for help and reading the Bible, I believe as it says in 1 John "We know that we live in him and he in us because he has given us his spirit." Jesus said, "On that day you will realize that I am in my Father and you are in me and I am in you." Jesus also said, "The Kingdom of God does not come with your careful observation, nor will people say here it is or there it is, because the kingdom of God is within you."

If we recognize that God the Father, the Son, and the Holy Spirit are one and His presence is dwelling within us and not out there somewhere, it is a divine gift. It may be the greatest gift God has ever given me. It helped me to understand God. It transformed my relationship with Him.

To Understand God Is to Love God

I found in Matthew:

> "'Love the Lord your God with all your heart and with all your soul and with all your mind.' This is the first and greatest commandment. And the second is like it: 'Love your neighbor as yourself.' All the Law and the Prophets hang on these two commandments."

God is love, in John Jesus says:

> *"Dear friends, let us love one another, for love comes from God. Everyone who loves has been born of God and knows God. Whoever does not love does not know God, because God is love. This is how God showed His love among us: He sent His one and only Son into the world that we might live through Him. This is love: not that we loved God, but that He loved us and sent His Son as an atoning sacrifice for our sins. Dear friends, since God so loved us, we also ought to love one another. No one has ever seen God; but if we love one another, God lives in us and His love is made complete in us."*

It helped me to learn that:

> *"We love because he first loved us. If anyone says, "I love God," yet hates his brother, he is a liar. For anyone who does not love his brother, whom he has seen, cannot love God, whom he has not seen. And he has given us this command: Whoever loves God must also love his brother."*

In this complicated world we live in, learning to understand God, we can find peace as He tells us in Philippians.

PEACE

"Rejoice in the Lord always. I will say it again: Rejoice! Let your gentleness be evident to all. The Lord is near. Do not be anxious about anything, but in everything, by prayer and petition, with thanksgiving, present your requests to God. And the peace of God, which transcends all understanding, will guard your hearts and your minds in Christ Jesus. Finally, brothers, whatever is true, whatever is noble, whatever is right, whatever is pure, whatever is lovely, whatever is admirable—if anything is excellent or praiseworthy—think about such things. Whatever you have learned or received or heard from me, or seen in me—put it into practice. And the God of peace will be with you."

For me, part of understanding God is the realization that he is the source of all peace.

MY PRAYER

Dear Lord I thank You for the gift of life and of all creation. And knowing that God's love is dwelling within me. I love You with all my heart and all my soul and I humbly lay myself before You in sublimation to Your will. I am thankful for this day You have given me to serve You. I pray that I can in my prayers, be alone with You in all Your glory. I pray that I can develop deeper skills of communication with You through prayer. And to feel the Holy Spirit abiding in me and that Your love and direction and Spirit is dwelling within me. I yearn for Your call to direct and guide me so that I can do for others as You would have me do for them.

Thank You dear God for sending Jesus Christ to reconcile the whole world to You through a beautiful rainbow of colors of love, joy and peace to shine upon us as we express our gratitude for the teachings of Your Son and our thanks for the gift of one more day to serve You. May we see the world and all the people in it through the eyes of Christ, think with the mind of Christ, love with the heart of Christ, and understand with the compassion and tenderness of Christ. Let me pray and walk with Christ all this divine day. As we walk as one among those who need us, direct me Dear God; guide me as you let me walk with you and your Son Jesus. I pray that You will dwell within me and I will respond to Your call.

DOING GOD'S WORK

———•◦•———

*M*y life changed when I started going to meetings with my sponsor and doing all that was necessary to maintain my sobriety.

Recovery is a spiritual program if you believe God is your higher power. I do. After years of searching for God's plan for me, I began praying for knowledge for His will for me with new hope.

I met alcoholics from all walks of life. All with the same incurable disease, whose lives have been completely out of control. Some homeless, some wealthy, some who had been sober for years and some there for their first day. This disease is a great leveler. We alcoholics understand each other's pain and share our guilt and frustrations. We are there to help each other. I had found a new purpose in my life. I prayed for the courage to carry it out.

The magnitude of the problem is staggering. Where ever I go and I say that I am an alcoholic, invariably someone will tell me about a friend or family member who is struggling with alcoholism. It is estimated that there are between 18 and 20 million alcoholics in America today and 40 to 50 million other victims, such as families and friends. In the U.S. someone is killed in an alcohol related accident every 30 minutes.

Our world is full of people whose lives are in shambles because of alcoholism: drunk drivers, suicides, failed careers, broken marriages, and children who will live in turmoil forever. Within the Fellowship we are all considered equals and there to help each other.

I know in my heart this is not the end of my spiritual journey. It will continue with God's help and because of the spiritual awakening I experienced with my sobriety. I know that I am called to carry the message to other alcoholics and help them find sobriety one day at a time.

In doing God's work and finding God I spent weeks studying and praying. I wrote this prayer and meditation to grow and expand my spirituality with others.

Prayer and Meditation

Begin by relaxing, taking some deep breaths, opening our hearts, minds, and souls to let God's love in as we:

Breathe deeply, feel the stress, anxiety, and anger drain from our body.

Humbly put our faith and trust in our loving God.

Quietly recognize God's presence our lives. Breathe in love, breathe out anger.

Breathe in peace, breathe out despair. We pray that we may be at one with God.

We have asked for His direction; we will accept His call. We believe we are where He wants us to be.

We accept where we are and who we are. Accept things for just what they are. There is no hurry. God will take care of things.

He has blessed us in so many ways.
(Acknowledge blessings.)
He will continue to show us the way.

Stop for a moment, breathe quietly, and accept
the presence of God.

Be humble; be grateful for God's love.

We pray for your love so that we may share
it with others.

We pray for peace so that we may share it
with others.

We pray for humility so that we may share
it with others.

We pray for forgiveness so that we may share
it with others.

Relax, take some deep breaths, and accept
the presence of God.

We pray that we can love God with all our hearts, all our souls, and all our minds. We pray that we will love our neighbor as ourselves. Do unto others as we would have others do unto us. Love others as Christ loved us.

We pray that our lives may be a window through which God's love may shine. We pray that we can expand our circle of caring and our ability to love.

Gracious God help us to be pleasant, loving, kind, be gentle, and be patient. We pray that we will be understanding, compassionate, nonjudgmental, and helpful.

Dear God we pray that we will have the courage to put our lives in your hands.
We pray that we will be thankful for your directions and blessings.

Our priorities are our lives with God and our sobriety.

Accept God's help, smell the roses, and listen
to the music.

Thank you God for every moment.

We know you will continue to show us the way.

I have shared this prayer and meditation with friends
and read it aloud to small groups many of whom have
asked for copies to share with their family and friends.

I have personally set aside an hour each day to
quietly participate in it with God.

———

A friend from a prayer group started an Easter Sun-
rise Service for members of our country club. The
morning was beautiful. Chairs were set up on a large
lawn; there was beautiful music, nearly 300 people attended. I was asked to give the closing prayer, which
I wrote and delivered. I was humbled by people's
comments afterwards. Some asked for copies of it. I
have been asked to do the closing prayer again this
coming Easter.

MY EASTER PRAYER

*We pray that we will humbly and lovingly answer
the call of Jesus Christ—as we pick up his cross
and follow him—open our hearts and minds and
souls and listen to the many ways he loves us—his
pleas for peace— his forgiveness—his understanding—his compassion—his kindness, gentleness
and patience—his caring—his guidance and
his direction.*

*We pray that we may love others as
Christ loves us.*

*We pray that we recognize the sins for which god
sent Christ to redeem us—as Jesus says, 'prune the
dead branches from the tree and we will be forgiv-
en.....as long as we have forgiven others, we pray
that we follow the teachings of Jesus Christ, believe
in him, commit our lives to him—and when our
time comes we can give our cross to someone else
and follow the risen Christ to heaven, eternity,
and everlasting life.*

A PATH TO FOLLOW

Every morning I start the day with my prayer and meditation. I ask God for directions for the day and how to find a way to achieve my original goals in life…to help others and make the world a better place. In many ways I have had a wonderful life and much to be grateful for even though the broad road was full of potholes, turns, and the obsession to drink. I believe that was God's way of showing me the path to follow. Finding God again at eighty-five years old, to the extent that I have found Him, reveals that it is never too late. I believe that I found sobriety at the time in my life that God planned for me.

I'm at peace, content, and looking forward to tomorrow.

I don't know whether it is my prayers, my writing, the time I spent in meditation, helping others, or just God being a strong source of light in my life but I have left the road that led to destruction behind.

"Enter through the narrow gate. For wide is the gate and broad is the road that leads to destruction, and many enter through it. But small is the gate and narrow the road that leads to life, and only a few find it."

I have found it—it's what I do with it that matters.
It's never too late.

EPILOGUE

I am very fortunate to have Dr. James West as my sponsor in recovery. He was one of three founders of the Betty Ford Center in Rancho Mirage, California. Jim had been a successful surgeon in Chicago before retiring and becoming the Medical Director at the Betty Ford Center. He is extremely well educated and dedicated to helping other alcoholics. I believe God led me to him. After completing the required steps, with Jim's encouragement I began sponsoring other alcoholics, helping newcomers and friends from the program.

I wrote a little book entitled *Finding Inner Peace During Troubled Times.* It was inspired by something someone said in one of our meetings.

I discussed inner peace with my spiritual advisor Bill Power. We discussed how difficult it is to find lasting inner peace when worried about the economy, wars, floods, hurricanes, and all the turmoil that exists today. The world is hungry for peace.

Finding Inner Peace During Troubled Times is successful in that friends bought copies to send to their families, friends, and employees, and it is available on Amazon. There are 25,000 copies in circulation and interest continues.

Chuck Colson's Prison Fellowship has sent several thousand copies to prisoners. I have received more than a hundred letters from inmates expressing their appreciation.

The Salvation Army has distributed approximately 10,000 copies to people in Texas, New Mexico, and Colorado. Five hundred chaplains at Fort Hood have received copies of the book.

After reading my book the president and founder of New Life Ministries asked if I would appear on New Life Live. I have been on the program three times and have been invited to do more. It is a call-in radio program with over 180 stations around America, with a potential audience of more than 2 million people. People who call in with life's problems are referred to one of 900 licensed counselors. Each of those counselors and some of the callers have received a copy of *Inner Peace*.

In addition to my work with the recovery of other alcoholics it has been a pleasure to write *It's Never Too Late*. I pray that God will bless this book and others will find it helpful.

I am continuing to expand and study prayer and meditation with my friend Dr. James Finley. I met Jim Finley, a former monk, who had studied with Thomas Merton at the Abbey of Gethsemani monastery in Kentucky. Dr. Finley wrote, among other things, *Christian Meditation: Experiencing the Presence of God*, a book primarily based on his association with Thomas Merton.

I thank God daily for Dianne. I am convinced she is an Angel. I would not be where I am today had God not brought us together. Our lives are happy and full. We enjoy our marriage, our many friends, and the life we have together in our Texas and California homes and in our travels. We continue to grow spiritually. Dianne is active and engaged serving as a Presidential appointee on a federal board, managing an employee scholarship fund she founded, and assisting the Mid-East Anglican Diocese.

I continue to write and study, and with God's help, continue my work with other alcoholics. I am content, happy, and at peace. I will be forever grateful for my recovery, the special and loving friends I have made, and the life it has given me.

God is doing for me what I could not do for myself.

Index

Citations

Matthew 7:14; Matthew 7:7-8; Colossians 3:5; Colossians 3:7-10;
Colossians 3:12-14; Colossians 3:15-16; Psalm 23; Ephesians 2:8-10;
1 John 4:13; John 14:20; Luke 17:20-21; Matthew 22:37-40;
Page 13 from "Finding Inner Peace During Troubled Times";
1 John 4:19-21; Philippians 4:4-9; Matthew 7:13-14

All Bible scriptures in this book refer to the
NIV (New International Version) Bible.